The Places I Love to Poop On

to Poop On

Written and illustrated By
Boaz Gavish

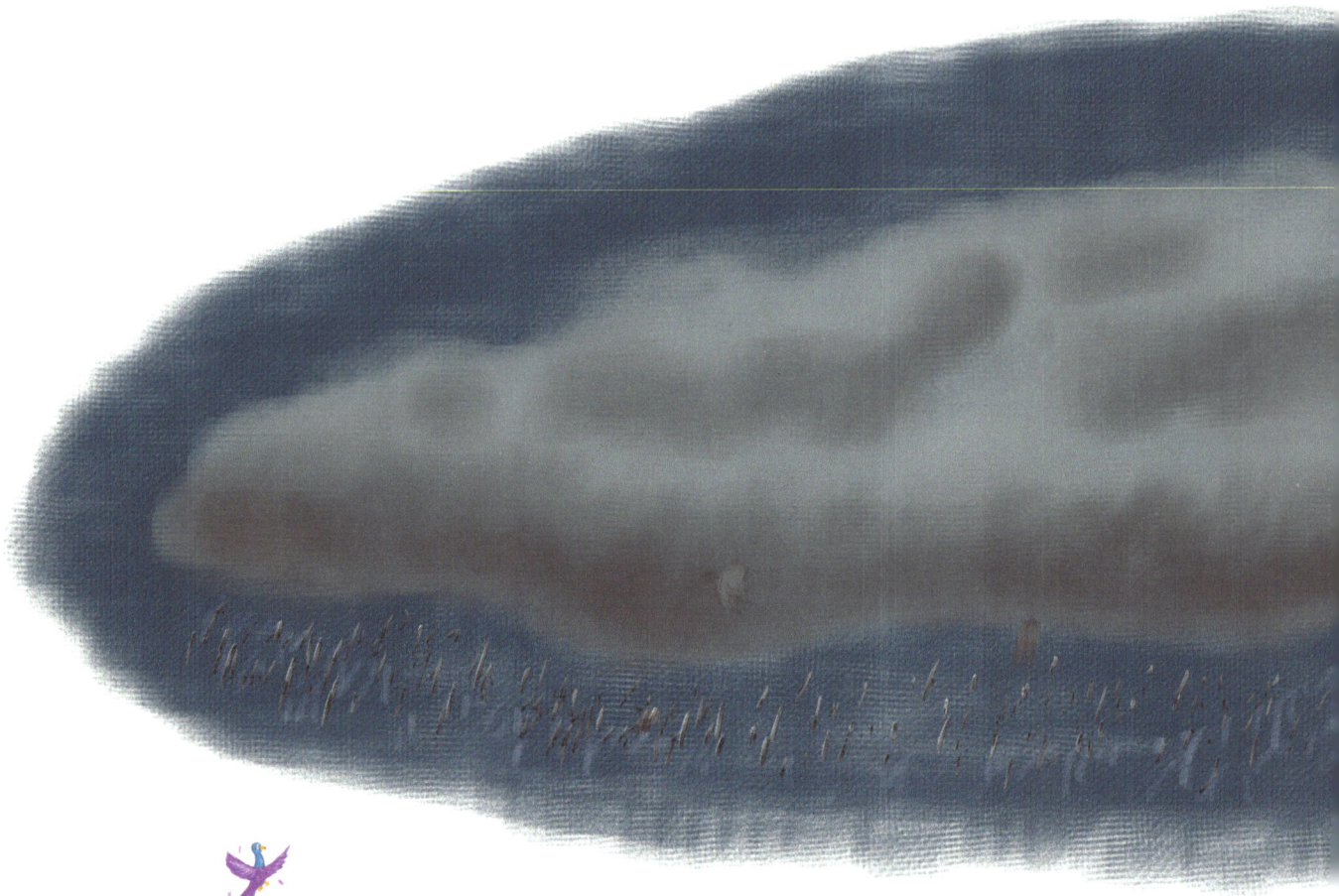

ISBN: 978-1-9997532-0-7

Book Cover by Boaz Gavish

Illustrations by Boaz Gavish

First Edition 2025

Special thanks to Jimmy Gleeson for his magical touch.

The Places I Love to Poop On

Written and Illustrated by Boaz Gavish

I'm Peggy the pigeon
and today I am sad.
The cold rain and wind
make me feel wet and *MAD!*

I know what to do!
I'll make my own rain,

so those down below
can share in my pain.

All these buildings are so pretty.
Very soon, they'll be my potty!

Look out for my surprise!
Let me give you a clue.

It's not number one.

It's my famous number two!

HA! I DO NOT EVEN CARE.
THIS ARCH JUST DOES NOT MIND
THE SQUISHY SPLIT-SPLIT-SPLAT
THAT COMES FROM YOUR BEHIND!

It's coming
toward your head.
I really have to poop!

POOP AWAY, MY FEATHERED FRIEND,
BUT YOU WON'T SEE ME FROWN.
A LITTLE POOP, MY DEAR,
CANNOT BRING ME DOWN!

And not long after that,
you'll feel my stinky squish.

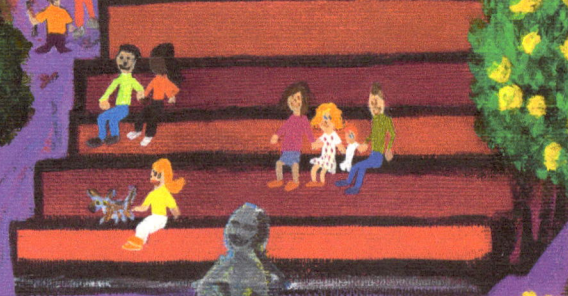

When things fall down upon me
from high up in the sky,
be it rain, or pigeon dookie,
or rotten custard pies,

I still feel so very happy.
No, me, it doesn't bother.
I will wear your poop
as a smushy badge of honor!

Your silver spire, so high and bright,
looks like it needs a topping.

Your poop is quite unpleasant, but it won't make me sad.

I'll imagine it's a present and make good come out of bad.

That cold wet rain, it made me mad,
made me feel upset and sad,

so I thought it would be fun
to rain on buildings from my bum!

But nobody was bothered,
no, it didn't darken their day!

They laughed, smiled, and shrugged it off
and continued with their play.

Neither rain nor poop is good or bad.
It's Just What happens, you know?
To feel better right away,
let it go, let it go, let it go!

Hello down there!
My pooping's at an end.
I'm sorry for the things I did.
Now let's all be happy friends!

www.ingramcontent.com/pod-product-compliance
Lightning Source LLC
LaVergne TN
LVHW072115070426
835510LV00002B/71